I Am Living Proof

WRITTEN BY MARILYNASHLEY PERRY

I Am Living Proof

Copyright 2013, MarilynAshley Perry
ISBN: 978-0-9899786-1-3

Scriptures were taken from The King James Bible, The NIV Bible and The Message Bible.

This book is dedicated to the people that held important roles throughout my life thus far. I have become a good woman because of you. I love you and I hope this accomplishment makes you proud; because of you I was able to write, inspire, encourage, and motivate others by letting them know that they can overcome any obstacle and be whatever they desire to be in this life.

Mom, Dad, Doss Family, Tonda L. Daugherty, Evelyn J. Belser, D. W. Bogle, Teianna Cooper, Jeanette Johnson and Bishop Marvin E. Donaldson, Mr. Kennedy, Ms. Cameron, Mr. Vance, Mr. and Mrs. Dennis.

Especially to my husband, who loves me in spite of all that I have been through. He is the reason I was able to complete this endeavor. He loves me, he completes me, and he enhances my very being. De'Mont Dionne Perry, I love you and YOU!

I AM LIVING PROOF
TABLE OF CONTENTS

I AM LIVING PROOF
TABLE OF CONTENTS CONTINUED

There were so many times in my life when I was troubled, tormented, hurt, confused, filled with hate and anguish. I was molested and abused. I was a drug dealer then later an abuser of drugs, alcohol and my own body. I was living life in the fast lane. In this book you will read about my journey. A journey that tore me, broke me, and tried to destroy me. You will observe the wrong turns I took, and circumstances that led me to the path I am on now – the path to my destiny. My journey began on January 14, 1983. When did yours?

MarilynAshley Perry

Chapter 1

MY CHILDHOOD

"Even a child is known by his doings, whether his work be pure, and whether it be right. The hearing ear, and the seeing eye, the LORD hath made even both of them."

Proverbs 20:11-12 KJV

I was born on January 14, 1983 at the rise of the crack cocaine epidemic. People were phasing out of the hippie stage into the era where free basing was now the thing to do. My mother was an addict when I was born and she moved around like a gypsy. Her roots were in St. Louis but she would settle in Kansas City where I was born.

She was part of the crowd that partook in some of the most infamous drug crimes known to Kansas City. Mom moved drugs around for dealers, used and abused them and befriended my god-mother. God-mother later became a snitch and had to be moved out of the state in the witness protection program. She was a key witness against one of the most notorious drug kingpins in Kansas City's history.

This was the Life that I had been exposed to at birth. I was in and out of crack houses with my mother. Sometimes I slept outside in the back seat of her car, while she was getting high inside the house. I recall going to and fro to unfamiliar places, with unfamiliar faces. I remember one particular time on an adventure with my mother, she and several other adults that were with us gave me and the other children some money to go to the store. This gave them time to get high. Although I didn't know what was going on, I understood that it was not right, and that I was hurting, sad, and felt abandoned and neglected. Upon returning from the store I gave my mother a rose I bought with the money. More than anything in the world, I wanted her to know that I loved her. If that was what it would take for her to come from these uncomfortable places, then I would rather spend what was for me on her. I wanted to show her that I cared.

Many times, I was left in the supervision of strangers – at least they were strangers to me. They were acquaintances of my mother. I didn't want to be around them. All I know is that I wanted my mommy. I would cry for days missing her and wanting to be with her.

I was left in the care of one of her friend's daughters, who would in turn leave me in the care of her brother, who I would later learn as my molester. He was a pedophile, who had some form of retardation, but he was mentally capable of making me, a 5 year old child, perform oral sex on him. I would gag and almost vomit every time. I believe this went on for a year or maybe two. It seemed like forever. I tried to block it out but was not able to do so, and I was terrified to tell my mommy. I thought I had done something wrong.

I remember going back and forth to my abusers home, where I would cringe and cry and throw a fit about being there. I couldn't believe no one knew, and this girl would continue to leave me in the hands of her perverted brother. This was just the beginning of being molested by males that were much older than I was.

My mom was in and out of rehab for the next couple of years. We moved to a suburban part of town called Grandview because my daddy wanted me to be raised in a better community that provided excellent education. He and my mother had been married since I was a year old. At the time he was an alcoholic, but he soon kicked that habit. He worked nights so I rarely got to see him, but when I did, I was a happy child! I remember he would always buy me a Snickers bar and I wanted him to have the first bite each time. One day that all changed. He was diagnosed with diabetes. I didn't understand why he would no longer take the first bite of my candy bar. In a way it crushed my little soul.

This man was not my biological father, but he was my daddy, and I loved him then and I love him now. My biological father was a mechanic in St. Louis who loved my mother, but didn't have the financial means to support her and her acquired lifestyle. He made a lot of promises that he did not and could not keep; he still makes those promises till this day.

I was troubled, taunted, and had been tainted by what I had seen, heard, and been exposed to. The spirit of perversion was on me and that damned devil tried to destroy me with molestation and incest. At the age of seven my older cousin began fondling me every time I visited St. Louis or when he would visit Kansas City. I had two different friends that had teenaged brothers that would do the same thing, so I thought it was normal. I shared it with one of my close friends who finally told someone what had been happening to me. It stopped one of the teenaged boys but not the other one. At ten years of age this is what my life had been inflicted with.

My mom finally got clean from drugs and alcohol, but I was dealing with the aftermath of my primary years and not being nurtured properly. At the age of twelve I had taken interest in a boy who made me feel pretty and special, so I willingly had consensual sex with him. He was sixteen at the time. I should have been playing with dolls, but I was sleeping around with a boy who was four years older than me. He was old enough to drive and I wasn't even in middle school.

That's when my life really began to go downhill. I became a runaway, I was angry and I was rebellious. I began selling drugs and setting men up to be robbed with my boyfriend who was abusing me physically, mentally, and emotionally. I was terrified of him, but I also loved him - even after he tried to burn me up in an apartment. My relationship with him led me to darker places. I was pretty and shapely for my age. I was eye catching but I was also devious, and bitter. I began being more promiscuous after I was no longer allowed to be with my boyfriend. My daddy shot him when he wouldn't leave me alone, as a parent he had had enough.

I began prostituting. It had been subliminally encouraged by my mother. She told me if I was going to be having sex then the least I could do is get paid for it. So I did. I stripped for money at private parties. I had even let a preacher perform oral sex on me for money; a preacher that my mother knew. He was the same one that married my parents when I was a baby.

I started dating girls and hanging out in nightclubs. Sometimes if I didn't have a ride I convinced my mother to take me. I was introduced to smoking weed. I went to prom with a girl to prove to everyone that I was going to do what I wanted to do. Nobody could stop me from doing anything. In my mind I was grown, but I was barely sixteen years old.

I later began dating a Jamaican drug dealer, who loved me but he loved his money more. He adored me, but he adored his money more. He honored me, but he honored his money more. He respected me, but he respected his money more. He was ten years older than I was and he began to school me and take me under his wing. There was nothing that he wouldn't do for me - financially at least. He was intelligent, he was arrogant, and he was one of my strongholds.

I loved him the best that I could, for a girl who didn't love herself. I thought highly of him and spoke well of him, but I spoke of him to the wrong people. Unaware of what I was doing, I confided in a guy because I thought he was cool, but he was really a snake waiting to bite. I placed myself in a predicament that was detrimental with my "savior". That was the problem; the

Jamaican had become my savior. He would speak things to my spirit which made me depend and rely on him. No matter how much I tried to move on, I couldn't. For some reason I would always run back to him. He was poisonous to me. His venom came off sweet, tasty and contagious, but he was separating me from my destiny.

Chapter 2

OUTCAST

"For I will restore health unto thee, and I will heal thee of thy wounds, saith the Lord; because they called thee an Outcast, saying, This is Zion, whom no man seeketh after."
Jeremiah 30:17 KJV

One of the hardest things for me to except is that I'm an outcast. Being an outcast as defined in most people's vocabulary is someone who stands out from the norm or their common group of people. I guess it is hard because an outcast is one who is rejected or cast out. Rejection is a challenging thing to deal with. Being born my mother's only child, I was a bold, outgoing and a fearless one. I was daring and never scared of anyone or anything. I always seemed to stand out no matter where I was.

In Elementary school, teachers paid special attention to me. When I was in my earlier years I had to have a pathologist, because I had a speech impediment. I also had a tutor for math in and out of school, but I always excelled in other areas of study. I have been an outcast since I was old enough to remember. Always outspoken and intelligent, my way of thinking was not the average child's way of thinking.

I always like to talk and write. One of my educators recognized this when I was in the fifth grade. She would take extra time with me, showing me patience that I needed, but I was a very troubled child, because of what I had been through. I always wanted to be different and I don't know if that's because I was looking for attention or because I was often misunderstood. Whatever the reason, I always seemed to stand out from the norm.

When I was in middle school the school administration wanted to try a new educating method. They developed a school called New Learning Community Center in Independence. Other students and I came from all over the metropolitan and surrounding suburban areas. We were teens and pre-teens that had many issues. My peers were already experiencing their own drug addictions, doing everything from shooting up, to huffing paints and gasoline.

We came from all types of homes. Upper, middle, and lower class neighborhoods were represented, but we all had one thing in common: we were outcasts from the normal educating environment. This was my first encounter with children who were similar to me.

When I was a freshman in high school, I returned to the school district where I lived. I had my tongue pierced and by then I already had two tattoos, which isn't unheard of today, but back then it was a big deal. I often got angry and didn't know how to control my frustrations in school, so I would be very belligerent and disrespectful. I was always the first student finished with my assignments in class, which left room for me to get into trouble. Even though I was an intelligent child, my behavior caused me to be labeled as being bad.

One day I got into trouble as usual - but this day was different. I was lied on by a substitute teacher who misunderstood me. I was always very outspoken and with that same boldness I always told the truth, even if it got me into more trouble. I was that child that just said whatever was on my mind. There is nothing wrong with the truth, but there is a time and place for children to speak. I always seemed to miss one or the other.

I got in trouble and was put out of the class, so I became angry. I wanted to get my belongings and go home. The teacher tried to keep me out of the room by holding the doorknob so that I could not enter the classroom. I was on the outside of the classroom and she was on the inside of the classroom. We were in a tug-of-war for the door. Being the bright child that I was, I decided that I was going to let go of the doorknob. If you know anything about pulling and forces, then you can only imagine what happened when I let go of that doorknob; she flew backwards and fell!

I received a ten day suspension from school for my actions and had to go on a trial before the school board. They decided to give me 180 days out of school. This was my freshmen year in high school. The year that most kids develop new friendships, get involved with sports, clubs and extracurricular activities. I was being kicked out of school for something that I didn't even do! The teacher lied on me and said that I pushed her down, but I hadn't. My mom was heartbroken and disappointed, although she knew I wasn't guilty. She knew I told the truth, but because of my past record of being disrespectful and violent with students who angered me, they expelled me.

I was in and out of alternative school settings from there on until I graduated from high school. Although this could have set me back, it didn't. I was and always will be ambitious. I attended school and worked two jobs. Alternative school was the best option for troubled teens like me. It was a smaller environment and the teachers knew I had issues that were rooted from within. The teachers allowed me to use my strengths. It seemed like they actually understood me for a change.

I was an outcast, always doing something to stand out from the crowd. I attended my junior prom with blonde and pink hair. I wore a baby blue dress and clear shoes. That was how I expressed myself - through my hair. I would shave it, grow it, cut it, weave it, bleach or color it. I always wanted to change my appearance to be different. I had the appearance of confidence, but I truly was battling with self-esteem issues. I liked standing out, but sometimes for the wrong reasons.

In spite of all the adversity that I faced with my education, I maintained a 3.4 grade point average and graduated a semester early. I walked the stage with my senior class of 2001. They tried to throw me away, but the drive that was in me caused me to strive for greatness and arrive at success.

I am an outcast for many reasons. It might have started off because I was rebellious, strange, peculiar, belligerent, outspoken, a know it all, or just too smart for my own good. I now understand that my conversation is different for a reason. I am known for being optimistic. My presence changes the atmosphere, and my smile is contagious. I think and respond differently than the others. My conscious mind doesn't even calculate information in the same way as others. I can't help it – that's just my nature. I am peculiar, sometimes talked about and often misunderstood. I am an outcast.

Chapter 3

LOOKING FOR LOVE IN ALL THE WRONG PLACES

"If I speak with human eloquence and angelic ecstasy but don't love, I'm nothing but the creaking of a rusty gate. If I speak God's Word with power, revealing all his mysteries and making everything plain as day, and if I have faith that says to a mountain, "Jump," and it jumps, but I don't love, I'm nothing. If I give everything I own to the poor and even go to the stake to be burned as a martyr, but I don't love, I've gotten nowhere. So, no matter what I say, what I believe, and what I do, I'm bankrupt without love. Love never gives up. Love cares more for others than for self. Love doesn't want what it doesn't have. Love doesn't strut, doesn't have a swelled head, doesn't force itself on others, isn't always "me first," doesn't fly off the handle, doesn't keep score of the sins of others, doesn't revel when others grovel, takes pleasure in the flowering of truth, puts up with anything, trusts God always, always looks for the best, never looks back, but keeps going to the end."

1 Corinthians 13:1-7 MSG

Where do I begin? This is not a boy, or girl thing, it's not gender based at all. This is a people thing. Love. We all need it; we all deserve it, and most of all we have to have it. What I have discovered is there are numerous ways that people cry out for love. I have also found that it is a necessity in life, just like food or shelter. We need love.

I needed love. I needed it so bad, that I didn't care where it came from. I was in a long term relationship with the boy my daddy shot from the age of twelve to fifteen. I allowed him to abuse me repeatedly and I would do anything he asked or told me to do. I lost friends behind my love for him. He was violent and ultimately I also became the same way. From this experience it was hard for me to try having a successful relationship in my adult years.

11

I've always loved harder or more than the person who professed to love me. I was in and out of relationships with multiple people at a time, because I feared being hurt, but I was always hurting myself. I equated sex and love together at one point.

I dated a guy once who was a Christian. He was older and he was a nice guy. He was in college, he worked, and he was just sweet to me, but I couldn't respect him being the genuinely nice guy that he was. That wasn't normal to me. This guy wanted to be celibate and that was not something I was used to. I had a different outlook on love, because I had never known what love truly was. I dogged him and it wasn't intentional, I just didn't know any other way.

I always fell for the one who was no good for me, but the ones that were, I was no good for them. It was a cycle and it was just beginning, I continued in it for years to come. This cycle led me into various places, even into promiscuity. What appears to be love might very well be the total opposite. Deception is common when the appearance of love is present.

There was another guy that really liked me. He was settled - a homebody. He had no children, his parents had been married for over forty years, and most would say that he was a good candidate for a potential husband. He loved me, but as always I had a bad boy on the side who was the opposite of him. No job, no car, three kids, two baby mommas, living with his cousin in the basement. He was mean, rude, and not a one woman's man, but he excited me more than the homebody, hardworking one woman's man, with a job, and stability. I remember looking that man in his face and telling him that I liked him. I also liked to party and I didn't want to hurt him, because I couldn't be the woman he needed. I chose the bum in the basement who I loved because his sex was good and he smoked weed. Since I was a pothead that was what I preferred.

He was a grimy person though. He was a thief, a liar, and a cheater, but I loved him just like my first relationship I was in at twelve. I found myself proving my loyalty for love. I would do almost anything. His cousin was dating a dope dealer from Chicago and decided to send ten thousand dollars cash to Kansas City for my dude (not my boyfriend, just someone I was sleeping with) to buy some cocaine for him. My dude had a different plan. He decided to steal the money. I was so frightened, but I loved him with his "up-to-no-good" self.

After that happened, I helped him flee to Texas, where he was supposed to stay until things calmed down. I should have known then if he would risk his own blood and family's lives, that he would risk my life too, but I was looking for love in the wrong place. When we arrived in Texas, he decided that he wanted me to be his girl, because he saw that I loved him. That presented a problem. I had a Jamaican that I loved too for different reasons. Actually, I wanted to be with the Jamaican, but his line of work didn't allow him to have the time for me that I desired. That's why I started messing with this crazy man from Texas in the first place. We started off as smoke buddies and eventually I started liking him. He had time for me.

Frequently I had pillow-talk with him, which is dangerous when you are sleeping with multiple men. I never had intentions on being with this boy from Texas. I had my own car, a job, my own place and I had no children, but he wanted to make me his girl and the Jamaican didn't have the time. So I moved from my place into a place with the guy from Texas. I went to work while he stayed home. I guess an idle mind is truly the devil's workshop. All while he was at home he was plotting; he and another one of his thieving friends.

What he was planning I would have never imagined, and if I could take back the days of me giving him information that would later be used against a man that put time, money, knowledge and energy into me I would. I was in a love triangle. I loved the boy from Texas because of his sex, he smoked, and I thought he had potential. The Jamaican I loved because he was intelligent, his conversation was like no other, he took care of me, he wined, and dined me, he was much older than I was, and he was like a daddy to me. He schooled me, and he was like no other man that I had ever dated. He had a lot of money. He's arrogant and powerful, he expected the best from me, and he's not your average "boss".

When I got home from work this bum wanted to rob the Jamaican. He knew the love, respect, and adoration I had for this man, but by this time I had already shared entirely too much information with him. It went down! I was terrified. I was confused. I no longer wanted anything to do with this boy from Texas, and I couldn't believe he had done the unimaginable - he robbed the one that I loved the most, and now I was in the middle of it all. The only way he knew of the Jamaican was because of me being naïve and confiding in him. He placed me in a predicament to test my love and loyalty for him through his dirty ways that I was once attracted to. He turned the tables on me and touched the man that I loved more than him, and he knew it. Jealousy is as cruel as the grave.

We went our separate ways because of this. I was not able to stay connected to him. I was so ashamed of what he had done and I didn't know how to tell the Jamaican that I was the reason this perpetrator had stolen from him. He wasn't stupid though. He inquired, and I talked to him in second and third person because of the guilt and shame that I felt. If I would have kept my mouth shut - better yet, if I would have just been content with our arrangement - I wouldn't have even been in a relationship with the other guy. He had put me in a dangerous place. This was my love life; it was full of deceit, multiple relationships and selfishness.

The Jamaican had many women, but I was his favorite, but that wasn't okay with me. I wanted to be his one and only. He would always tell me, "as long as you are taken care of it should not matter" and "as long as the others know your place with me and don't disrespect you" it doesn't matter. That is what he meant and that was a hard pill to swallow. This is how I managed to date him for ten years and have multiple relationships, because he already had established that he wasn't getting married until he was fifty years old. I subjected myself to this life for ten long years and could never have a successful love life because anyone I dated knew of him, and felt threatened by him. They knew they could not have me in the entirety because my heart was really his. I was not content with this arrangement. I always wanted a husband, children, and faithfulness to exist.

The danger in looking for love in all the wrong places is we might not know what real love is. Because of this, I subjected myself to pretty much anything. Even when love looked me in the face I was in no place to embrace it. I had refused to accept love and I didn't believe that it was real. I had a relationship with two different men, one to support me emotionally and spend time with while the Jamaican would be on business trips. The Jamaican supported me financially. I did not trust either of them. I couldn't be trusted either at this point I had been through and seen so much, that it left me as a prisoner in my own body.

The man who supported me emotionally loved me, his eyes lit up when he saw me, he was sweet to me, he was kind, he was funny, he was protective and he was sensitive to my needs. I didn't understand why. I questioned his motives. Why did he take pride in me? Why did he have adoration for me? Why was he nice to me? Was this genuine? Was it possible for someone to actually love you with no other intentions? I doubted his constant actions of love toward me because of insecurities and the fear of rejection and abandonment. I was not receptive to the love shown toward me, which is another reason I thought there was more security in having multiple relationships - because I always anticipated the worst. This was all I knew, but I desired to know something other than what I had been complacent with for so long.

Many times I acted out of my fears instead of embracing faith and love. I pushed people away. I put on a shell trying to protect myself. I didn't have control as a child and I thought I would at least have it as an adult woman. I was protecting my heart. All while trying to protect mine, I hurt his. This was my final lesson it was after him that I learned love never fails. Eventually my ten years invested would come to an end with the Jamaican. We had a great friendship and could talk about anything. There wasn't anything that he would not do for me, but I realized that I had to love myself more and to set my standards for what I truly desired - a loving marriage, not one that I would have to share myself or my husband in the name of love.

Some people have ulterior motives that might produce the image of love on the surface, but in depth it's malicious and derogatory. Control is another false hope in the concept of love. Some may believe because someone is trying to control them that that is their way of showing love. That is a lie. There are several kinds of love, but deception, control and lust are not forms of love at all.

One form of love is STORGE. This is the love displayed within a family. It is likened unto the love of a parent to a child, or a child to their mother or father. It is a loyal love towards friends and community and required virtue, equality and familiarity. Philia is the affectionate regard or friendship type of love. It is a dispassionate virtuous love; a platonic kind of love shared by comrades. Agape love is used in the biblical passage known as the "love chapter," I. Corinthians 13, and is described there and throughout the New Testament as sacrificial love. It describes the feeling of being content and holding one in high regard. It is a love filled with various virtues including patience, kindness and gentleness. Eros is the more passionate love, with sensual desires and longings. Coupled with agape, this is the love that is shared by a husband and wife in the sanctity of marriage. It is an appreciation of the beauty within a person, and becomes the total appreciation of their beauty. Unconditional love has no limits.

I can surely tell you that most of the times that I thought I was loved or in love, I didn't fully understand the total concept of love. Not until I met my husband, the love of my life. He began to show me a whole new meaning of love and forgiveness - which work together. He said something powerful to me when I told him that I had fallen in love with him. He said, "Don't fall in love. Walk in it". I was confused then, but now I understand. Maybe you will get it one day, if you don't get it now. When you fall usually it's down. You get hurt and you have scars, but if you walk you are moving forward together, hand in hand with the one you truly love.

Chapter 4

PROMISCUITY

"Having therefore these promises, dearly beloved, let us cleanse ourselves from all filthiness of the flesh and spirit, perfecting holiness in the fear of God."
2 Corinthians 7:1 KJV

I was having one night stands after one night stands, religiously. I was having sex constantly like a chain smoker smokes cigarettes. Sometimes I would have sex with two or three men in one day. I would have sex with partners, even a husband and wife together, or two men at once. Sex was no longer something that mattered to me. It was just sex. It wasn't intimate, it wasn't personal, nor was it sacred. It was just sex.

I would have sex with people whose name I barely knew. I wouldn't enjoy sex, I would just have it, or should I say it just had me. I would just participate, it was no longer pleasurable. I was empty, I was numb, and I had no cares. I was dangerous. Sometimes I charged for it and sometimes I didn't. It just depended on how I felt at the time. Sometimes I used condoms but most of the time I didn't. I used sex as an outlet to express my hurt, my lack of commitment, and to get cars, money, drugs and things I wanted or whatever I felt like I needed at that time. I would have sex anywhere with anyone.

I remember when I wrote this chapter and I started to type it up, I was so ashamed, disgusted, and hurt that I committed these acts that I was once relentless about. Promiscuity is real and I know I am rare and unusual especially being willing to admit that I was a whore. I would pick up people's habits and didn't know why. I would get into my feelings about someone I laid with, and then go and lay with someone else to get that person off my mind. I did that continuously, but it never worked. I was smiling on the outside, but I was truly crying on the inside, and I needed help, but didn't know how to get it. The promiscuity I had been dealt was a generational curse.

Lying down with man after man and woman after woman, I was wounded and continued to reopen my wounds as I opened the doorway to my womb. One in, one out. Another in, another out. Catching sexually transmitted diseases and headed to the clinic once again. I was scared out of mind - is it going to say positive this time? If it does will I even remember all the names to give for those they should call to be tested? The sad thing is I didn't know them all, nor did they know me, my background or where I came from. I experienced the feeling of emptiness that still existed after lying in a wet bed. What felt like pleasure was really causing me pain.

I felt anguish, frustration and loneliness. I had an incomplete feeling. There was still a need, a want, a desire that over took me – lust - and it tried to take me out on a number of occasions, too many to even recall. I had to share this in order for me to be free from the shame, the guilt, and the condemnation that I had after putting myself through this lifestyle of promiscuity. The life of whoredom, fast living, lying down with individuals that I was not married to was a sin to myself, committed in the flesh and against Almighty God.

1 Corinthians 6:18 says, "Run from sexual sin! No other sin so clearly affects the body as this one does. For sexual immorality is a sin against your own body." [NIV] For so many years I had been misled and redirected on to another path; usually the wrong path. I became numb and it didn't even matter anymore. I no longer had a preference just sexing with people to be doing it.

This demon is real and perverted. It had me doing the unexpected, unimaginable, and the worst things possible. There were times I woke up the next day and said, "I can't believe that I did that with that person." I tried to escape the truth to create a false truth, but in doing so, I also created enemies. I was having sex for money, clothes, shoes, cars and other material things that will all pass away, but my soul is to remain forever. My soul was damaged because of sin.

That lust demon was never satisfied. It always wanted more, and more is what I gave it. It resided within me and caused other things to begin to flee from my sight. My vision didn't seem to get any clearer because not only did I have my natural eyes to look through to see what God was trying to show me; I now had John and Jane Doe's eyes as well. My vision continued to get blurry as I opened up my inner self to a dark dying world.

Even the Bible tells us that when you lay down with someone you become one with them; it is very clear in 1 Corinthians 6:16, "What? know ye not that he which is joined to an harlot is one body? For two, saith he, shall be one flesh." These words were very true in my life. I had become one flesh with many that I laid with. I remember going to the clinic one time. There was an illustration on the back of the door showing one person then two people being together sexually. Then one of the two slept with another person so it was 1+1=2 and 2+1=3. So in reality, although one of those people had only physically experienced intercourse with one person, they actually laid down with their partner's other partner too. The illustration went on and on adding the numbers and multiplying. That was showing me God's Word all along, I just didn't know it at the time.

I believe your virginity is a promise, something sacred that should be assured to one's husband or wife. I wish I would have kept mine. This is the very reason I believe the enemy used lust to attack me I was tainted at a young age. I didn't know how to protect myself from this perverse spirit, or how to recover. Its approach was cunning, slick, smooth, and sometimes even tasteful. It set up shop in my life and I had no idea how to control it, so instead it controlled me. I was able to acknowledge its very presence knowingly and unknowingly. Sometimes it had me doing things that I knew were not okay. I was complacent and made lust acceptable. How dare that damn devil and his demons come in and play mind games with me.

There are more things than sexually transmitted diseases to be concerned about. While suffering from promiscuity, the other STD's to be plagued about is SPIRITUALLY TRANSMITTED DEMONS. I was what I laid down with. There were so many insecurities created and weights placed on me. I was emotionally and mentally scarred. I had health issues and heart issues. Thank God I never tested positive for HIV or AIDS. It created issues in my relationships, not just with people I was dating, but with my friends and family as well. Sex is influential and it should be in its proper place. These impure immoral things that existed in my life are nasty, careless and provided no health benefits. It caused greed, jealousy, envy, and it desired attention. Yes I was promiscuous. I'm not proud of it, but I am no longer ashamed of it either. I am living proof that you can overcome whatever evil influence is plaguing you.

Chapter 5
SLEEPING WITH THE ENEMY

"How long must I wrestle with my thoughts and day after day have sorrow in my heart? How long will my enemy triumph over me? Look on me and answer, Lord my God. Give light to my eyes, or I will sleep in death, and my enemy will say, I have overcome him, and my foes will rejoice when I fall. But I trust in your unfailing love; my heart rejoices in your salvation."
Psalms 13:2-5 NIV

I was sleeping with the enemy. Drug dealers, murderers, lust-filled homosexuals and drug addicts were all my enemies. Sometimes the very thing that you fear will start to come after you to kill you. I was attracted to people with a murderous spirit. In fact the attraction was so strong that it was also attracted to me. I could tell if you had killed before, and if you had my attraction toward you grew. It excited me in an odd way.

I remember taking a walk in Loose Park with this guy and I stopped him, looked him in his face and said, "You're a killer." He looked back at me and said, "How do you know?" I said, "I can see it in your eyes – I like it." He looked stunned. He later went to jail for a quadruple homicide.

I dated men that were not secure within themselves and they always tried to tear me down. I was involved with individuals who could care less about my wellbeing. A lot of times, I was my own worst enemy. My insecurities and lack of self-worth influenced my poor decision making; decisions that mostly were not in my best interest.

My boyfriend from Texas that was a thief definitely was my enemy. He put me in danger on many occasions, and even after I had no contact with him, he was a repeat offender. He broke into the Jamaican's house again and tried to kill him. The Jamaican hid from me that he had been shot. I found out from my mother. He told my mother, but told her not to tell me, because he didn't want me to worry. She slipped and told me anyway, and when she did I felt it in my gut.

I knew who had done this. Almost a year later, he had contacted me and I told him that I knew it was him because he was murderous, jealous and envious. Although he didn't want me, he did not want anyone else to have me especially the Jamaican who he felt inferior to. The sad thing is he never denied it when I asked him, he just asked me how I found out about it. Then he described to me how it went down and he confirmed my fear of him, that he was dangerous, my enemy, and out to destroy me. I foolishly let him back in my life. I had got involved in church and was trying to live right. Then we got back together and I got pregnant, but we fought so much that I miscarried.

He came back to finish what he had started, but I recognized the truth sooner that time and no longer allowed him in my bed. Now I had to fight the same demons off that came back with him to get me and catch me while I slept. I needed an awakening out of my false realities, my illicit dreaming. I needed to find out my enemies and see why they were after me. What was it about me that they wanted to be in my bed? Why was I the intended target?

My enemy tried to kill me by having me involved with drug dealers, killers, and lust-filled go getters. You should know your enemy so that you know how to tactfully defeat it. I know when you read or even heard the title "Sleeping With the Enemy" you couldn't help but to think of the movie about domestic violence, brutality, and malice, but what you have to realize is sleeping with the enemy is much deeper than those examples. It was beyond messing with my friend's man or them messing with mine. It was more than me laying down with a bottle of vodka and pills to cope, or sniffing powder up my nose, or even me staying busy not to face reality. When my thoughts were not pure, I began to entertain them, and that was when I begin sleeping with the enemy: myself.

All these things came from childhood, day to day activities, what I would watch, read, and listen to in conversations, music, dramas, comedies, are just examples of what we can all relate to. After all, my enemy may not be your enemy nor yours mine. I sometimes invited these unwanted guests to my home which is my temple, meaning my body. We are all three parts: mind, body and soul. Some of the things that I shared, I had never shared with anyone. As a matter of fact, I didn't plan on sharing it all but I had to expose the enemies that I had been sleeping with so that my sheets could be cleaned and I could rest peacefully again.

Chapter 6

IDENTITY THEFT

"Therefore each of you must put off falsehood and speak truthfully to your neighbor, for we are all members of one body. In your anger do not sin: Do not let the sun go down while you are still angry, and do not give the devil a foothold. Anyone who has been stealing must steal no longer, but must work, doing something useful with their own hands, that they may have something to share with those in need."

Ephesians 4:25-28 NIV

My identity had been stolen. I didn't even know who I was. I didn't know if I was coming or going. This became my way of life. I was hardcore on the outside - fearless and angry - but on the inside I was this little girl hurting, scared, and uncertain. Who I was meant to be was far from me and my understanding. I would just go with the flow of how I felt from day to day. I changed my hair so many times, length, and color from week to week, people could not recognize me if they didn't know me. Sometimes I would change my name, although I was already mixed with Irish, Italian, Indian, and Black, I wanted to be mixed with something else other than what I was mixed with.

If I found someone to be more attractive than myself I would try to pick up their habits or ways or even their style. From time to time, I would even try to talk with an accent, because I didn't like the way I sounded when I spoke. I walked around inferior because I was uncomfortable in my own skin. I was not content with who I was.

I was having a real identity crisis. It didn't help that I wasn't confident. On top of that I had no one to build me up or validate me. My worth had never been defined to me. From the time I could remember, I wanted to be someone else, thinking that someone else probably had it better than I did. They probably hadn't been molested. They most likely had a good relationship with their mother – unlike me. They liked being themselves, and I wanted to be them – or like them. Stolen identity occurs all the time.

My character was anything other than who I was meant to be, so I must have had an imposter. I was not producing for my own good, and that was self-destruction. When I picked up self-destructive habits it damaged me. I was infiltrated by something other than Godly attributes. I believe that my true identity had been stolen, and I was a victim of identity theft. I had to ask myself who my traits identified me with. I had been robbed of my identity at a young age, and was all over the place trying to find what had been taken from me. I lost my identity all while trying to find it, and I wanted it back.

Chapter 7

HOMOSEXUALITY

"Don't you realize that this is not the way to live? Unjust people who don't care about God will not be joining in his kingdom. Those who use and abuse each other, use and abuse sex, use and abuse the earth and everything in it, don't qualify as citizens in God's kingdom. A number of you know from experience what I'm talking about, for not so long ago you were on that list. Since then, you've been cleaned up and given a fresh start by Jesus, our Master, our Messiah, and by our God present in us, the Spirit."

1 Corinthians 6:9-11 MSG

I had my first girlfriend in the ninth grade. I liked her cause she was more understanding than men. I went to the gay clubs and it was a small little world from the regular community. I dated her for a few months, and then on to the next, she was just a few years older than me so I would hang with her and other adult women who lived their lives as lesbians. I was attracted to girls. I thought they were pretty, but mostly I thought we were precious jewels, and men could not value or appreciate the worth of a woman like we could as women. I continued dating women all through my high school years.

I began dating this girl from California. We were the same age. She had long hair, but she dressed and acted very masculine. Even though I called myself liking girls, I only dated masculine women. I would still try and make them feminine, telling them to wear panties instead of boxers, make them wear skirts, and even get their hair done, but that never worked.

It was our senior year. She went to Blue Springs and I attended Grandview Alternative School. We met at a basketball game, she was walking past me and I told her she was cute, so we exchanged numbers. We hung out daily from the fall up until the summer of graduation. I went to prom with a girl because I wanted everyone to know that I was gay. I rocked the female symbols, rainbow necklaces, and earrings so that everyone would know that I liked girls. She had not told her family, although they already knew we were proclaiming to be best friends. This was odd, especially since we had only known each other for eight or nine months. Prom came and I went with her so that I could prove that I was in the lifestyle. We took pictures together. She had a tux on and I wore a two-piece dress from a fancy boutique.

We left prom to go get high, popping ecstasy together and we just lived our lives freely. She introduced me to ecstasy. That lifestyle was very wild and off balanced for me. I had convinced myself that I was going to marry a girl one day. I even attended church with my girlfriend from time to time. I dated girls who were obsessed, crazy, erratic, and obviously emotional. I had encounters with friends that escalated into mixed emotions and misunderstandings. My childhood friend started messing with the first girl that I had dated, behind my back. The homosexual lifestyle had just as much drama as the heterosexual relationships that I had been in before.

Being gay for me wasn't really about sex it was mental, and it was about the friendship. It was the fact that I thought women were gentle and could relate better to me since I was a sensitive person. It was a soap opera! Every week someone had a new boo and was so in love, then two months later the same thing happened all over again. Although I justified my liking girls because I had been through so much with males in my life, I thought it was absolutely disgusting for men to like men. That was gross to me. What a one-sided way to be. I remember seeing one of my classmates down at the club Soakie's, and he had some high heels on. I always knew he had homosexual tendencies, but he confirmed it this day, it was odd for me to see him down there.

I was an adult and still in the lifestyle, but had decided that I was still attracted to men. I moved in with a roommate - a girl - who too was promiscuous and liked girls. She watched porn on a daily basis. The next thing I knew, I began watching porn regularly. She had men and women in and out of our apartment and so did I. This would be my final year dating women. The last girl I dated happened to be the cousin of the guy from Texas. In fact that is how I met him. She was an ignorant broad. She had a five year old son, and when she would come to spend the night she would bring him with her. That made me feel so uncomfortable.

I wouldn't want to hug, kiss, or for her to say anything inappropriate to me in front of him. When we slept in the bed together she would try to hold me but I would put him in between us. It was starting to be gross to me and not feel so normal. Even though I had been dating girls for several years, I realized that I was not gay and that I didn't want to operate like a gay woman in front of a child. I started thinking that if I had children I would not want them to be gay.

I still know a lot of gay people. My classmate that I had seen that time at Soakie's died from AIDS when we were only twenty-four years old. Even though I had been hurt by men, I had also been hurt by women. So I was no longer going to try to live a certain way because of hurt, that was just an excuse.

I tried many things that were the opposite of most people because I wanted and tried hard to be different. I liked the attention whether good or bad. I introduced this homosexual lifestyle to a few good friends of mine, and I hate that I did that. This was one of many phases that I went through in my life. I was confused about being a homosexual and it caused confusion. That's why I believe women dress like men and men dress like women. Homosexuality is loud, flamboyant, and has a need to be seen. It is a liar. It lies to people by trying to convince them that they were born that way and that they are alright with how they are. If this were true, they would not take so many measures to prove to themselves or others that they are gay and alright with the lifestyle.

That demon messed with my natural feminine ways as a woman. It tainted my natural perception of what sisterhood really is. That lifestyle for me was not balanced or stable. It was another form of perversion for me. I had been looking for love in all the wrong places, sleeping with the enemy while being promiscuous. I dabbled in homosexuality while experiencing identity theft. It wasn't the lifestyle for me, so I continued searching for who I really was.

Chapter 8
CHARACTER

"Cultivate these things. Immerse yourself in them. The people will all see you mature right before their eyes! Keep a firm grasp on both your character and your teaching. Don't be diverted. Just keep at it. Both you and those who hear you will experience salvation."

1 Timothy 4:15-16 MSG

My character often was someone wild, fun, spontaneous and always unpredictable. I was very loud, rude, outspoken and disrespectful. I liked to fight and I was one who didn't like bullies. I wasn't going to start anything, but I would definitely finish it. I'm a sweet person and I like people, but I wasn't one that you would want to cross or get on my bad side. I could be very vindictive and spiteful. I always wanted to help people, but most of the time I extended a helping hand to the wrong people.

I've always been one to wear my heart on my sleeves. I've always talked too much. I couldn't hold water if I had a bucket. I was always mature for my age. I grew up really fast, I liked to dance, laugh and play. I was always outgoing, and willing to try anything at least once. I enjoyed partying and having a good time. I liked meeting new people.

My feelings are easily hurt and I am easily offended, and although I say what's on my mind, I never really wanted to hear what was on someone else's if it was going to hurt my feelings. I am very giving, but selfish at the same time. I was very independent and usually rode solo. I only had one or two friends.

Building your character is never a job you ask for or purposely searched for. It just comes along with the territory of being born and going through the motions of life. Character building started at birth. Being molded by the people who raised me, I took some of their qualities and flaws knowingly and unknowingly. I believe that is where the saying "the apple doesn't fall far from the tree" comes from.

My character is my overall being. It is my makeup. It is who I am. It is what I really am on the inside and not what I might appear to be. As I have matured, my growth has become visible. Even though some people pretend or choose to be blind to it. I strive daily for maturity to take place and for continued character building.

Chapter 9

DON'T BE COMFORTABLE WITH
THE DEVIL USING YOU

"Be sober, be vigilant; because your adversary the devil, as a roaring lion, walketh about, seeking whom he may devour:"
1 Peter 5:8 KJV

I have invited the devil in to sit on my couch. Once I was old enough to know the difference from right or wrong, many times I still opted to do wrong. Giving in to my own wants or what I thought I may have needed was not always in my best interest. I used drugs consistently for some years, and I didn't always have the best judgment. I even sold drugs a few different times. I would exchange crack for money, never looking the dope fiend in the face.

I had a little trap house. I would give the man some crack to use his small quiet secluded home to sell crack out of. I never sold drugs for any of the drug dealing men I had. As a matter of fact, they didn't even know that I was attempting to profit by selling drugs. The girl I was dating from California left some cocaine in her safe, so I asked the Jamaican to cook it up for me so I could sell it and send her the money. I was ruthless and had a hard life, so I was not really interested if I inflicted the same hardships on anyone else. That didn't cross my mind. I had people trying drugs that they had never done, and because I was an influential person it wasn't very hard to get people to do what I suggested.

I had my friends stripping and prostituting, since it had worked for me as a way to make easy money. I enjoyed seducing people making them do what I wanted. It was an adrenaline rush for me to be able to control people or have some influence in their choices.

The reason I stopped selling drugs was, on the Fourth of July, I was getting ready to give this crack head some crack. Something spoke to me and said, "Look her in the face". She was trying to give me a plate of food in exchange for the crack. I told her I don't need food - I had food. When I looked at her, I saw children missing meals, missing their mother, and I saw me being molested because someone was selling crack to my mother when I was younger. I never sold crack again, I flushed it. I flushed all of it. That stopped me from selling crack, but it didn't stop me from using the Jamaican's money to support my own habits and lifestyle.

I would coach and help people who lived that street life. I continued to be used by the devil. The married man that had asked me to sleep with him and his wife knew that I took ecstasy and he asked me to bring a pill on the night that we had our rendezvous. He was going to drug his wife who did not smoke or drink. Her husband of fourteen years wanted to slip this pill into her drink - why I don't know - especially when she was willing to do whatever he asked her to do. Being the wild seductress that I was, I brought the pill, and I took her to the bathroom to put our lipstick on, knowing he was going to put this drug in her drink.

This was not the first time or the last time that I willingly let someone take advantage or encourage an alternative form of pleasure for someone. The more I pondered on things, the more those thoughts became my realities. I was comfortable with the enemy. Don't be comfortable with the devil using you.

Chapter 10

FOOLISHNESS AND IGNORANCE

"As a dream when one awaketh; so, O Lord, when thou awakest, thou shalt despise their image. Thus my heart was grieved, and I was pricked in my reins. So foolish was I, and ignorant: I was as a beast before thee."
Psalms 73:20-22 KJV

I know I have done many ignorant things in my foolish days. Getting in the car with strangers out of town, drinking and driving on a regular basis, even fighting people if they looked at me the wrong way, I overdosed on ecstasy and still continued to use drugs after I recovered from my near death experience. This is how I can speak on being ignorant, foolish, and intelligent at the same time. I chose to operate foolishly even though I was highly intelligent. It takes a smart person to act crazy. I had such a short temper and I would blow up without a second thought. Many times I just reacted without thinking. I would cuss you out and say all kinds of hateful things and did not care who I hurt. I was just ignorant.

I would be loud and make scenes. I wasn't scared to fight. I liked to fight - especially people who thought they were tough. I never believed in jumping people and I believed in fighting one-on-one with no weapons, just fists! I always kept a pair of tennis shoes in my car just in case I needed them. People I hung around knew I was rowdy and if someone started something they could call me to finish it. I don't think I intentionally looked for trouble but it always seemed to find me.

My ride-or-die was the same way. She wasn't loud like I was. She was very quiet, but would beat the crap out of somebody. We didn't care about who, what, when or where. If you brought some drama or nonsense to us you were likely to get dealt with. I always did dirt with her and no one else. She wasn't scared and neither was I, but that always got us into situations that were foolish.

Being hot headed and short tempered almost cost me my life several times. I would often drink so much that I would black out. One night I went on a weed run. I was so drunk that I didn't notice I had got a flat tire on the way there. All I remembered is flirting with him as I always did. He would usually just laugh and pay me no attention, but that next morning when I had woke up from blacking out something was different. I went to the bathroom and my panties were on backwards. I was confused. The weed man was in the bed that I had just climbed out of, so I went to ask him what happened. He looked at me so surprised. I had no clue as to what had happened after I got there. He had sex with me and I don't believe I was coherent. This wasn't the first time that I had been taken advantage of.

I would often drink heavily and blackout. Once before, when I was under-aged, I went to sleep drunk with one guy and woke up to another one on top of me. When I opened my eyes there was someone that I did not consent to having sex with penetrating me. I began screaming and hitting him, he got up and I felt so violated. I was made to feel like I couldn't call the police because I was wild and liked to party. Here was this guy that was on his way to college. Surely they weren't going to believe me. I didn't consent to him touching me but my drinking and partying had put me in that position. Who would believe me? The girl who was there with me didn't even believe me.

I continued to abuse alcohol to the point of blacking out. I was just foolish. I have so many instances where I was just being ignorant in my life. Many times my encounters involved others being ignorant too. Since my temper was short, I had many altercations with people, especially with women over men that I was involved with. When I had broken up with one of my many boyfriends, I decided that I didn't want anyone else to have him, because he was a good guy. Although I didn't know how to treat him right, I wanted him to still be there if and when I figured it out. So I would act a fool with any girl that he started dating, letting them know that I was crazy.

I went to this girl's house and tried to kick her door in. Once I ran her off, he got with another girl, who was just as ignorant as I was - if not worse. She was more childish than ignorant. She played on my parent's phone, so I thought that if I went to her house and acted a fool she would quit. I went to her house unannounced and acted a fool. When she came outside, I ran up on her and we started fighting. She was mad at him, but it didn't stop her from seeing him, or playing on my parent's phone. I continued to mess with him as well. I fought her another time after that. I finally decided that I wasn't going to fight her anymore, because it did not solve the problem.

The last time I went to her house, I decided that I was going to talk to her like I had some sense and try to catch him up, but when I knocked on her door, she wasn't there. His little brother answered the door, so I pushed my way through because I was angry. I marched up the stairs and he started running down the stairs to stop me. He picked me up, still in shock that I was there. I began hitting, scratching and punching him, and he dropped me on the ground. I was hurt - injured physically this time. I landed on the ground on my wrist and it was broken. All because I went to someone's house to act ignorant. He looked me in my eyes with the most remorseful look I had ever seen and said he was sorry.

It took me two years to let him and her go after that, but at that point in my life, I had made up in my mind that I no longer was going to be hot headed and short tempered. I would be a lady and a child of God. There has to be a point where drama should end, or at least my approach to it would have to be different.

When my face got cut I had just graduated from high school five days prior. I had several warnings and I failed to heed to any of them, because I was so bull-headed. I went to the place where the girl hung out on two different occasions. One of those times I went into the apartment summonsing her to come out and fight me. While I foolishly waited on her she left the scene.

I was upset because she had stolen my wallet and opened up a checking account in my name. She was writing fraudulent checks. I could have just pressed charges, but I wanted to dog her out and beat her down in the streets. I liked to fight and I felt like that was how you earn respect and taught people not to mess with you. Someone warned me when I told them of my plans to fight this girl. They told me to be careful because it was rumored that she liked to cut people because she couldn't fight.

I didn't listen. Twenty-seven stiches in my face and seven staples in my head made me understand how ignorant and foolish I really was. The things I knew for certain were foolish and ignorant were the very things I tended to do most of all. I smoked although I knew it caused cancer. I smoked because I wanted to do it. Drinking hard liquor causes organs to go bad and alters your speech, mind, and the ability to make good decisions, but I continued to be a drunk. I continued to have unprotected sex even though I knew the risk. These are all foolish and ignorant but I did it anyhow.

I have been guilty of talking too much and not listening and it is wiser to listen twice as much as you speak - after all you have one mouth and two ears. When I think of the foolish things I used to do, I am thankful that I did not die before learning how to operate in wise decision making. Maybe my mistakes can make a difference in a positive manner in other's lives, so that they don't have to go through the same ignorance and foolishness.

Chapter 11
DO AS I SAY, NOT AS I DO

"And ye fathers, provoke not your children to wrath: but bring them up in the nurture and admonition of the Lord."
Ephesians 6:4 KJV

I didn't really have the best examples when growing up. My mom did the best she could at that time in her life. I had some serious issues and lacked respect for her as my mother. I watched her go in and out of rehab. I watched her have many male friends, I even watched her mess with men who attended the church I was raised in, men that had wives, and men that were supposed to be ministers. Their wives spoke to my mommy, and I thought that was horrible. I couldn't say anything because I was a child. I was probably about ten when I recognized it.

Even though I didn't say anything I acted out because of it. She would try to correct me, then turn around and try to be my friend, which was confusing to me. As I got older I understood more and more what was going on, and it became even harder for me to obey my mother. She would correct me and I would say something back about her own actions and she would reply "Do as I say not as I do". That didn't work with me. I was a very outspoken child, and I was in a new era. I didn't respect my mother the way I should have.

She would pick and choose when she wanted to parent me and she really would not discipline me. When she started to discipline me she had already waited too long. I would fight back and I really felt like she couldn't tell me what to do because she did too much in front of me.

When I reached high school, I learned that she too had liked girls. She even had a girl living with us that was in her early twenties. She tried to be my friend, but at the same time wanted to have an authoritative role over me. By then I felt like my mother was more like a sister than a mother, and her example was far from maternal.

I didn't know how to take her or her discipline. It was like a joke to me. When my parents put me in counseling the psychologist tried to tell them their roles and the parts they played in why I acted the way I did. They wouldn't accept responsibility for their lack of parenting. Instead they tried to bandage my anguish with material things. My mom tried to keep me active in dance, girl scouts and other activities, but what I was missing was her. I wanted her to teach me how to be a lady, not a seductress. How to be a wife, not an adulteress. How to be honest, not sneaky or devious. How to exist in this world with integrity, being loyal and solid. I wanted her to teach me something different than what she taught me. It was confusing to me to get in trouble for acting a certain way, and I wasn't shown anything different.

It's not always the child's fault for acting up. Sometimes it's what's being taught in the home or the lack of discipline and love. You cannot expose children to bad and expect them to do good. Do as I say do, not as I do - in whose world? Not this one! My mom tries to show me right from wrong now, and I look to her for friendship. I want to be able to talk to her and get sound advice from her. I just want her to listen, hug, kiss, and encourage me. I wanted something real and I wasn't the type of child that you could be a hypocrite in front of. It just wouldn't work. I just needed and wanted to be led by a good example. I will always remember that the best way to teach a child is to lead by example and not by mere words. This is still a very commonly used phrase by parents and guardians in the home. The worst part is that it is used in Christian homes by Christian parents. The phrase is contrary to the Word of God in so many ways.

Chapter 12

FAMILY

"Now therefore fear the Lord, and serve him in sincerity and in truth: and put away the gods which your fathers served on the other side of the flood, and in Egypt; and serve ye the Lord. And if it seem evil unto you to serve the Lord, choose you this day whom ye will serve; whether the gods which your fathers served that were on the other side of the flood, or the gods of the Amorites, in whose land ye dwell: but as for me and my house, we will serve the Lord."

Joshua 24:15 KJV

The very first family was Adam and Eve and their children Cain and Abel. The "family" was jacked up from the beginning. That was not God's plan for us. Jealousy and murder took place, and if you keep reading you will see that Rachel and her sister also had some jealousy issues. So you see, it's not just in today's family, your family to be exact, that the problems occur. It has always been this way from the beginning of time.

I'm going to reveal some things about myself and my family in this chapter that will be uncomfortable for me to discuss, but it's real. Through these words, I expect someone to gain healing and deliverance. I suffered from incest, molestation, drug addiction, homosexuality, promiscuity and alcoholism.

Although I'm talented and have many gifts, these are the problems that I suffered from. They sometimes overshadowed the God given abilities that I possessed on the inside. The same gifts that would make me successful.

Sometimes my family exhibits mental conditions that cause nervous breakdown - an acute, time limited phase of a specific disorder that manifests primarily with features of depression and anxiety. We are not built to deal with the pressures of life and that is why we breakdown. Although I never had an actual break down, I have had anxiety and panic attacks on a number of occasions. That is part of the reason I used to smoke weed. It would keep me calm. Scientist and doctors probably have studies to prove some of the things that I am revealing. My evidence lies in my life experiences and repeated history in my family of certain behaviors, mind frames and patterns. For most that will be good enough, and for others that need further proof, I suggest that you take a look at your own family history and patterns whether it is good or bad.

I didn't choose my family. God predestined my relatives for me. Families are made of mothers, fathers, sisters, brothers, grandmothers, grandfathers, aunts, uncles, and cousins. Within families there are generations. In each generation, there are blessings and curses. Some families are knit closer than others. Some were born into the families, and some have been adopted or married into the family. Families are born with blessings, and some with curses. Either way, gifts come without repentance and so do callings. That's why you have families that are very successful in various fields; be it in politics, sports, music, or professions. Gifts, talents and callings generally run in the family. This is also true for curses that are on the family I can identify what they are in my families by recognizing a repetitive attribute that has history and has lingered through generations. I have learned to be honest with myself and acknowledge these negatives and positives. If they are negative I learned that I need to counteract it with the positive. If they are positive I need those qualities to be cultivated.

There are some known families, with known gifts and known curses. The Kennedy's are intelligent, prominent, well liked, and influential, but women, alcohol, and tragic deaths occurred in their lives at considerably young ages. The Manning brothers that play professional football are from a lineage of football players and they are probably preparing their son's to be their successors. I wish that people would have recognized early in my life what the good and the bad was in my family so that the good in me could have superseded that which was corrupt in me. Kansas City has a family that has had a history of murderers in their family and it was passed on through generations. These are just a few examples.

You read about my childhood in the first chapter. My first cousin molested me. He later raped me. That is when he identified that it was sick and wrong. He never touched me again and he wrote me a letter apologizing to me. I forgave him and I communicated with him, later finding out that he too had been molested by a male cousin in our family, and was sexually abused by a woman that was unrelated when he was a young boy.

My grandfather was an alcoholic and my uncles followed in those steps, they also abused and sold drugs. Now they are all sober, Glory be to God, but I see the same cycle afflicting my cousins; their sons - as it did me. I smoked marijuana for over ten years, but I also abused ecstasy, cocaine, prescription drugs, and alcohol. Even though I despised it and it had caused lots of pain in my childhood, I still fell victim and prey to my family's curse.

My grandmother was a sweet woman. She was well-liked and most importantly a highly respected woman. She didn't play games and she didn't take any mess from people. She especially didn't play when it came to her children. She was a real grandmother. She tended to all of her daughters when they had their children. She even came to Kansas City when I was born to help my mother with me. She died when I was thirteen years old, but the memories I have of her are full of love. We have family stories that keep her memory alive. I appreciate the love, morals, and the independent abilities she placed inside of her children. I have a loving family. They are funny, excellent cooks, and love to serve people. My family is filled with the most giving, hospitable people that I have ever met. They are celebrities in their own right, very popular, and well liked.

I wish I had grown up in the same city with my family as a child, however I am overall thankful for my family especially my mother. We have had our share of hardships, heartaches and problems, but most importantly, we've had positive attitudes towards life and we never give up! Even though I am not as close to them as I would like to be, I truly honor, respect, love an appreciate all of them. I love my family. There is nothing like family!

Chapter 13

ABANDONMENT AND NEGLIGENCE

"Hide not thy face far from me; put not thy servant away in anger: thou hast been my help; leave me not, neither forsake me, O God of my salvation. When my father and my mother forsake me, then the Lord will take me up."
Psalms 27:9-10 KJV

I was abandoned as a child leaving me hopeless, scared and with the mindset that I was unwanted. I was mishandled often in my primary years by the very ones who were supposed to nurture me. I was neglected, being left in the hands of many different people even my abusers. Issues that come from abandonment will scar you. I often cried for my mother begging her not to leave me. Abandonment caused issues in relationships and created unhealthy habits. I feared and lacked trust in individuals who genuinely loved me because the people who should have loved me neglected to do so, and neglected to protect me from abuse.

Negligence from my biological father also scarred me. I couldn't grasp the reality of what a good man was, because I had not had much to go off of. I remember after turning twenty-two, my biological father decided that he wanted to have a talk with me about men and how to carry myself as a woman. It was a nice gesture but he was ten years too late. My daddy who raised me was a provider, but that was all. My parents neglected to care for me properly and encourage me in the foundational stages of my life.

I was often scared and when my mom would leave me to go off on her binges I would cry feverishly for her, wanting to be with her. This was traumatic for me. I was left with people to raise me at different periods in my life, but not for long. My mommy always came back for me. This was the beginning of many psychological and behavior issues that would take place later on in my life. This form of abuse caused me to have fear and uncertainty in life. Several insecurities also developed.

I found myself being clingy to people, men and women trying to fill a void that was never fulfilled through childhood. These very things followed me into adulthood and I had terrible friendships. I often allowed people to use me, because I desired friendship so bad. I even had false families, because of the need to be wanted or to belong to someone. Although I was never in a gang, I can understand how people get involved in them. It's the need to be validated by people because you haven't been approved or established at home. It will make your search for that in the wrong areas. I always had a play cousin or sister, even though I was an only child. I was always adopting new family members.

My clinginess might have come off as overbearing, possessive, or even as a form of jealousy. I was always very protective over my friends or those I deemed to be my family. I had issues and they began at a young age. I didn't want anyone to neglect me. It doesn't feel good to be rejected and abandonment is a form of rejection. It made me feel inadequate and all alone. I believe this hurt me more emotionally than anything else I had experienced.

Chapter 14

TRANSFORMATION

"Therefore, I urge you, brothers and sisters, in view of God's mercy, to offer your bodies as a living sacrifice, holy and pleasing to God—this is your true and proper worship. Do not conform to the pattern of this world, but be transformed by the renewing of your mind. Then you will be able to test and approve what God's will is—his good, pleasing and perfect will."
Romans 12:1-2 NIV

I decided to give my life to Christ. It was very unexpected. I just wanted prayer, but my heart was sincere and I wanted to change desperately. I just didn't know how. I got baptized and was filled with the gift of the Holy Ghost. When transformation took place, I began to see things I had never seen before. I began to feel ways I had never felt before, and things that didn't matter before began to matter. Things that did matter before were no longer a factor, but became a reality check of things I had not experienced yet. I recognized that being transformed was a process. It didn't happen immediately and it has good days and bad days. I was willing to wait on the Lord to help me through them all because "they that wait upon the Lord shall renew their strength; they shall mount up with wings as eagles; they shall run, and not be weary; and they shall walk, and not faint." Isaiah 40:31

It was rehabilitation for my mind, heart and soul. My whole outlook on life changed for the better. I could see things differently and more clearly. God showed me who I really was. He showed me where I used to be and even bits and pieces of where I was going during the process. I had fears and doubts that arose, but I had to stay strong. I began attending church on Sunday and bible study on Wednesday. I started reading my bible daily and really studying it. I began to pray more than just before bed at night. My prayers changed from "now I lay me down to sleep prayers". I learned how to pray. I even started fasting. I tried to intentionally apply what I was learning at church and in the bible to my everyday life. I had a change of heart and mind.

This was something new to me, but I wanted to try it. I mean after all, I had tried everything else. I heard the Lord, and he spoke directly to me. It tripped me out at first, I even thought I was hearing things or that it was my conscious talking to me, but it was transformation taking place.

I wanted more of this transfiguring to take over in my life, so I began to keep God's Word and his promises in my heart. Keeping him first and staying at his throne, seeking his face as well as his grace and mercy. My faith began to surpass the fears that I had from this change. A change that was inevitable. I had to keep in mind for a "brand new me" transformation was a must.

Even Christ transformed before a select few of his disciples. I read in the New Testament [Romans 12] "Be not conformed to this world but; be ye transformed by the renewing of your mind." Change starts in the mind. So I decided not to be scared to go through the metamorphosis, but to trust God to see me through it. I started learning and understanding his Word, so I understood that God is not a God that will start a task and leave it incomplete. If He starts it, believe He will finish it!

Chapter 15

LONELINESS

"Be careful for nothing; but in every thing by prayer and supplication with thanksgiving let your requests be made known unto God. And the peace of God, which passeth all understanding, shall keep your hearts and minds through Christ Jesus."

Philippians 4:6-7 KJV

This is definitely a common emotion people face at one point or another in life. Loneliness is especially common to those who have suffered from abandonment or negligence in their life. It's a fear of being left and being all by yourself. I have finally come to the understanding that you may be lonely but not alone. People have always stated that to me and I always felt so alone. I wanted to be able to physically see someone, and touch them, because I am a see it to believe it type person. My god-mother would tell me, "every time you desire a man or someone to keep you with some type of companionship desire God that much more." I mentally tried that, but my heart wasn't in it.

My thoughts were more like "I'm still lonely and I want to be married with kids". I even was having thoughts like "you're married of course you can say that, you have someone you can lay next to and laugh with and tell deep thoughts or desires to", not recognizing that I did too: God of course. Before I came to the realization of how real and true that actually was, I allowed myself to be in a position where I settled for something that was not in my Father's plan for my life.

The enemy is so crude that he sent me just what I thought I wanted. I should have guarded myself. Since I was now being transformed. I should have dismissed all feelings and yielded to the Holy Spirit. Even though it didn't feel good to be alone, it was good for me at the time. Just like some foods that are good for you, don't always taste good to you. Sometimes emotions can lead you to sin, which is what separates us from God. Sin starts to take place if you ponder on it long enough. Eventually you will act on it. I was emotional and even though I had given my life to Christ, I was still lonely. I still wanted someone to laugh with, lie with and share common desires with. The enemy knew this because of me speaking these things aloud. I would always say how lonely I was.

I am a young woman of God, called to evangelize and prophesy. Here comes a young man who is attractive, close to my age, an entrepreneur dresses nice - not like a thug, but with a hood mentality, and book smart. He started attending church with me with no arguments. As a matter of fact, we never argued. He would attend bible study too. We shared a lot of things in common, which was important to me. Our common interests were the icing on the cake - so I thought. We were both our mother's only child. One of our parents smoked crack together, and we were both molested. We were writers and cared about the generations after us. Sounds good right? Wrong. You are probably thinking what could be wrong with that? He sounds like the perfect candidate right? Wrong!

God gives us spiritual gifts for a reason. To use them. There is always a warning before destruction. I ignored the signs. I had seen who he was and the enemy was using him as a distraction. I dreamed it, seen it, and one of my friends called him a wolf in sheep's clothing. That is as plain as black and white right? I was still lonely, and he does go to church. He does whatever I ask, so God you can change him. You changed me and He will see that I mean to do your business so he will follow suit too right? Wrong again. People have to desire to change and not operate with ulterior motives. Sometimes people don't even know that they are being used by forces that are evil. We are free moral agents, and God has a plan for a reason. He created me. He loves me, so why didn't I trust him to do His job? Although He knew my desires and he promised me that he would give me the desires of my heart. I still didn't believe Him.

I had to learn how to get out my feelings, so that I would be effective in my prayer life and my walk for God's Kingdom. I could not be effective having a pity party for loneliness, so I had to blowout the candles and put the food up because nothing was going to come out of it. I got rid of him, but they kept coming the following year.

I had to experience some unnecessary hardships from marrying the wrong person. All because I wanted to rush God to give me what I wanted. He was schizophrenic and bipolar. Clinically crazy and he tried to kill me, but God covered me. He woke me up in the middle of the night calling me "Zephaniah". I heard the name two more times so when I looked up the meaning of the name it said "God will hide and protect". God did just that for me. I had to shake that spirit of loneliness that caused me to get impatient and settle for less. I searched for scriptures to keep me and help me stand on God's Word, but most of all I allowed God to come in like never before.

Chapter 16
MIRROR, MIRROR

"For if any be a hearer of the word, and not a doer, he is like unto a man beholding his natural face in a glass: For he beholdeth himself, and goeth his way, and straightway forgetteth what manner of man he was. But whoso looketh into the perfect law of liberty, and continueth therein, he being not a forgetful hearer, but a doer of the work, this man shall be blessed in his deed."
James 1:23-25 KJV

Mirror, Mirror on the wall, what will I see when I see you looking at me?

My cousin had me to look at myself in the mirror as a project. I recommend that you do this project as well. I had looked at myself a thousand times before in the mirror. Sometimes to check for boogers, pimples, to make sure there was nothing in my teeth, to do my hair, to put on makeup or pluck an unwanted hair. For whatever reason you have looked in the mirror, I assure you this project will be different. I'm going to be very honest; I did not want to look in the mirror. I did it for a moment because I didn't like what I saw. I decided to do it later when no one was around. I had to look at my inner being. I had to look into my own eyes and into my own soul. This was the first time I, MarilynAshley, had looked at myself. I saw what people see when they look at me. Most importantly, I saw a firsthand view of my characteristics.

Self-examination was getting ready to take place, and it was taking place internally. I acknowledged my features: thick eyebrows, freckles, full lips, and a cute little nose, granddaddy's ears, daddy's teeth, grandmother's smile, and mom's light brown eyes. I looked at myself and my conscious started talking to me saying, "I see you, but who are you?" It was at that point that I realized I didn't know who I was. I mean of course I knew my name, date of birth, social security number, where I was born, and my hobbies, but I didn't know myself. I never took the time to spend time with myself to learn who MarilynAshley was.

So when I finally gathered enough courage to look at myself in the mirror, I saw a young, smart, beautiful girl - a girl that had been angry, abused, hurt, and mishandled. I saw all of my good and my bad. I began to cry. I saw myself as a child being abused, then as an adolescent abusing myself. I saw my early adulthood phases and I cried even more. As I cried, I began to stare at myself in that mirror and face every hurt, every attack, every failure, self-worth and esteem issues. There was a release and a cleansing. A great healing began the day I looked in the mirror.

I kept staring at myself, but this time I started smiling. Then I began talking to myself through my conscious, telling myself how beautiful I was and how fortunate I was. I began valuing myself at that moment, and I made a conscious decision that I was no longer going to be affected by my past. I was going to befriend myself and work toward self-preservation and my endeavors. Mirror, Mirror on the wall, thank you for revealing to me my hurts, my pain, but most of all my strengths and my beauty.

Chapter 17

BEING NEW

"Now that you've cleaned up your lives by following the truth, love one another as if your lives depended on it. Your new life is not like your old life. Your old birth came from mortal sperm; your new birth comes from God's living Word. Just think: a life conceived by God himself! That's why the prophet said, The old life is a grass life, its beauty as short-lived as wildflowers; Grass dries up, flowers droop, God's Word goes on and on forever. This is the Word that conceived the new life in you."

1 Peter 1:22-25 MSG

The change was so dramatic that I was not even used to myself. I have become new. The bible says that old things are passed away and all things become new if you are in Christ. So old ways, old friends, old thinking, and old behaviors and actions are unacceptable. Old things actually made me uncomfortable. The things I used to do I didn't do anymore. I had grown past those things. Though my skin was still the same, my heart and my mind were changed. Transformation had again taken place! I had changed into something that I had never been before.

I stopped drinking, smoking, partying, clubbing, whoring, and fighting. All this was a process. It did not happen overnight. Although I wished that it would have. I backslid several times before making these changes permanent in my life. It was hard, but my heart, mind and willpower over took me, causing me to want better than what I had been previously producing. I had been in the midst of shoot outs. I overdosed on drugs and alcohol. I had been abused physically, mentally and emotionally. I had even had my face cut open with a box cutter, causing me to get twenty-seven stitches. None of these events that occurred in my life caused me to change. I was stubborn, rebellious, and didn't want to hear from anyone. I had a longing in my heart. My life was missing something, and I would not stop until I found out what that something was.

Being new is a state of mind. Being new is reflected in your actions. Being new becomes your persona. When you become new, old things are no longer supposed to exist in your future. Don't be mistaken, old things attempt to be present in your life. I have decided to use power and authority to make old things cease. The only thing the enemy has is my past, which I have been liberated from. My adversary wants to intervene with my being transformed and becoming new, but he can't touch me, because I belong to God. Since I am in God's hands I have allowed Him to make and mold me.

I have a new way of thinking, and since I think differently I respond and react differently when trials and tests come my way. God gets the glory in my new life. People have seen me being new and wondered what caused this transformation to take place. My only answer is - Christ my Lord.

Chapter 18

MEDITATION AND PRESERVATION

"Keep this Book of the Law always on your lips; meditate on it day and night, so that you may be careful to do everything written in it. Then you will be prosperous and successful. Have I not commanded you? Be strong and courageous. Do not be afraid; do not be discouraged, for the Lord your God will be with you wherever you go."

Joshua 1:8-9 NIV

Meditation is keeping the Word steadily before you according to the book of Proverbs. Joshua tells you to meditate on God's Word day and night. I will admit this has been a challenge for me. I was so use to always moving and never sitting still. I was used to being independent and making my own – often destructive – decisions. I was not accustomed to God preserving me. Preservation is being set aside, kept fresh or stored up for a purpose. That time finally arrived in my life. It was time to become preserved and fully consecrated with meditation.

Since I was single, I could spend more time with God and less with man - mankind that is. When this whole process started I had no idea that one day I would enjoy or even be interested in spending time with God. What I didn't know is that God had prepared me along the way. He allowed people I trusted to trash me. People I had once laid with and friends I used to pray with. They began to separate from me one by one. He started twisting and turning my ground and surroundings. I'm so glad he did!

The Lord woke me up out of my sleep to let me know that He is the only friend that I need. What a perfect time to find that out. Through meditation and preservation you become intimate with God and understand His Will for you. At that time your friend, Father, Savior and God is able to reveal himself even the more.

When you are meditating on the things of God, you are able to listen and hear his voice clearly. When I took time out to spend with God, I was being preserved while meditating in His Word and in prayer. It continually has me desiring to do His will.

The bible tells us to seek the kingdom of God and righteousness first, and then the things we desire will be given, so I continue to seek the face and voice of God. God grants certain rewards to those that diligently seek Him. Meditation and preservation helps me to examine and evaluate myself in areas of my life that need improvement. I have learned the process and value of waiting. Since I came into the knowledge of God, there is nothing stopping me from possessing all that God has for me. I can have what is rightfully mine: love, joy, peace, endurance and happiness. I have received restoration from all the time I lost sleeping with the enemy, while experiencing identity theft from that old lying thief - the devil. I run bath water. I turn on some worship music or jazz and I relax. I leave stress in the water and I come out refreshed and renewed. Let the words of my mouth and the meditation of my heart be acceptable in your sight, Oh Lord, my rock and my redeemer. Amen.

Chapter 19

FINALLY RESCUED

"But when I was down they threw a party! All the nameless riffraff of the town came chanting insults about me. Like barbarians desecrating a shrine, they destroyed my reputation. God, how long are you going to stand there doing nothing? Save me from their brutalities; everything I've got is being thrown to the lions. I will give you full credit when everyone gathers for worship; When the people turn out in force I will say my Hallelujahs."
Psalms 35:15-18 MSG

I remember the day God saved me and set me free from sin Hallelujah! I was at peace for once, and had found rest for my soul - so I thought. The process had only just begun. It was a long time coming but it finally arrived. My eyes had been opened to the things of the world that had been blinding me all along. As I write this, it sounds to me as if it was something that I had once read or heard from someone else. People could have said the same thing before, but it didn't make sense to me then. Now it makes perfect sense.

I was rescued from myself and the misery and agony of life as I knew it. I knew my mommy once had a problem; a problem that caused me to be in multiple places and started arguments between her and my father. I knew men had touched me when I was left alone with them. I knew that my friends' older brothers touched me. I knew my mother had many male friends and my daddy worked what seemed like seven days a week all year long. I knew that he wasn't my biological father, but he provided for me. My biological father always made promises of gifts that I never saw. Promises of a Nintendo, a trip to Six Flags, letting me live with him, and flying me to California to meet my grandmother. Those things bothered me then, but they don't bother me now.

I knew that I was smart. I knew that I could swim. I knew that no one ever expected my mother to give birth to me. I knew that by the time I hit adolescence that I wanted love. I knew I didn't want to do drugs or smoke cigarettes because they were bad. I knew that I was made to go to church and Sunday school. What I learned in church let me know that something was wrong with what I had learned at home.

I wanted attention so I got it from older boys. I lost my virginity at a young age. This experience opened up many Pandora's boxes. It seemed like the keys were thrown away and I was unable to close the boxes and relock them. I knew I was in danger - some known and some unknown. All the experiences life had given me taught me deceit, lust, rage, envy, strife, malicious and devious ways. Drinking and driving caused destructive actions to me and anyone else who I was involved with. I was careless and carefree, battling depression along with consistent tormenting thoughts and ways. I had become a prisoner locked up and jailed for my crimes as well as my family ties. I was always hurting and had a lot on my mind.

I wrote God letters and poetry from time to time telling him about my pain and misery and asking him to help me. Sometimes even asking him to end it. I felt used, abused, cheated, mistreated, overlooked and misguided. Although I was, God always put someone in my path that spoke hope into what seemed to be a worthless life - to me at least. God kept angels shielding and protecting me from being destroyed and killed. People witnessed to me when I didn't want to receive it.

I went to a few different churches and had some encounters with God. I still stayed trapped in a defeated state and did not embrace Him coming to rescue me. That's why I understand when people don't take the way out when God gives it to them. I'm grateful that God extended his mercy to me numerous times before I actually accepted His helping hand.

I got a job at a salon where I worked for two years. This lady witnessed God's love and compassion to me. She showed me that He was a provider of all things, but His love is what won me over and ultimately what saved me from my sins. To find out that He loved me this whole time overwhelmed me. At times it seemed too good to be true. He came for me when I least expected - when I was mostly no good and had disregarded Him. He came for me after being raped, molested, prostituted, a drug addict, a lover of money and a lover of those who didn't love or acknowledge Him. He still came for me. He rescued me more than once.

I got saved and I backslid a few times before I decided that there was no turning back. I had been rescued from sin that had me unable to think with my right mind. In order to live a life that would be pleasing to God, I had to be rescued from the darkness of the life I once lived. Yes, I was finally rescued!

Chapter 20
VICTORY FOR THE VICTIM

"Oh death, where is thy sting? O grave, where is thy victory? The sting of death is sin; and the strength of sin is the law. But thanks be to God, which giveth us the victory through our Lord Jesus Christ."

1 Corinthians 15:55-57 KJV

The best way to be victorious over your enemy is to know your opponent. Know their weaknesses and strengths and remember that they study you, so they know yours as well. You have to be on guard at all times. The bible tells us to put on the whole armor of God so that we will be able to be victorious over the tricks of the enemy.

"Finally, my brethren, be strong in the Lord, and in the power of his might. Put on the whole armour of God, that ye may be able to stand against the wiles of the devil. For we wrestle not against flesh and blood, but against principalities, against powers, against the rulers of the darkness of this world, against spiritual wickedness in high places. Wherefore take unto you the whole armour of God, that ye may be able to withstand in the evil day, and having done all, to stand. Stand therefore, having your loins girt about with truth, and having on the breastplate of righteousness; And your feet shod with the preparation of the gospel of peace; Above all, taking the shield of faith, wherewith ye shall be able to quench all the fiery darts of the wicked. And take the helmet of salvation, and the sword of the Spirit, which is the word of God: Praying always with all prayer and supplication in the Spirit, and watching thereunto with all perseverance and supplication for all saints; And for me, that utterance may be given unto me, that I may open my mouth boldly, to make known the mystery of the gospel, For which I am an ambassador in bonds: that therein I may speak boldly, as I ought to speak." – Ephesians 6:10-20 KJV

These verses helped me to counteract the enemy and overcome the obstacles that were brought into my life. I guard my heart and mind, which are my most valuable possessions. Keeping a clear line of communication with God through His Spirit, I conquer my tests and trials. I am victorious from my past, from sickness, from mental illness, from diseases, from family curses, from bad attitudes, from society, molestations, rapes, abuse, homosexuality, drug addiction, low self-esteem and whatever I had fallen victim to. I am free! I am no longer in bondage or held in captivity.

I am no longer a victim because I choose not to be. The things that I wrote about helped free me from all the hurt, pain, sadness and many other emotions which I faced because of my life experiences. I decided to have the attitude of a winner instead of one of the defeated. I learned to turn my negatives into positives. I learned how to be optimistic and to have joy no matter what situation comes up in my life. That's my attitude toward life. I am going to live it to the fullest, be thankful and use my time wisely while here on this earth. You only get one life, so why not make the best of it?

I refuse to have a woe is me attitude. I am an overcomer of many bad situations. I had no choice in some, but many I chose to be in. Overall I decided that I can do anything I put my mind to doing. I am a successful entrepreneur and licensed cosmetologist for over ten years. I am a college student working towards my Bachelor's degree in Mass Communications with a minor in Journalism. I am a good wife and soon to be mother. I love people, but most of all I enjoy helping people. Above all these things this is what makes me the most victorious! I've got the victory!

Jesus laid down His life so that we might live, so why should we continue to live anything other than a victorious and Godly lifestyle?

"If the Son therefore shall make you free, ye shall be free indeed." St. John 8:36 KJV

"Nay in all these things we are more than conquerors through him that loved us." Romans 8:37 KJV

"What shall we then say to these things? If God be for us, who can be against us?" Romans 8:31 KJV

"For the weapons of our warfare are not carnal, but mighty through God to the pulling down of strong holds; casting down imaginations, and every high thing that exalteth itself against the knowledge of God, and bringing into captivity every thought to the obedience of Christ;" 2 Corinthians 10:4-5 KJV

All I am saying is it is written that I am a winner, that I am an overcomer and that I am victorious. If you have the proper tools, knowledge, wisdom, and weaponry you will always prevail. I am living proof that you can be victorious!

www.ingramcontent.com/pod-product-compliance
Lightning Source LLC
Chambersburg PA
CBHW031225090426
42740CB00007B/716